Fennec Foxes

Victoria Blakemore

© 2018 Victoria Blakemore

All rights reserved. This book or parts thereof may not be reproduced in any form, stored in any retrieval system, or transmitted in any form by any means—electronic, mechanical, photocopy, recording, or otherwise—without prior written permission of the publisher, except as provided by United States of America copyright law. For permission requests, write to the publisher, at "Attention: Permissions Coordinator," at the address below.

vblakemore.author@gmail.com

Copyright info/picture credits

Cover, nattanan726/Shutterstock; Page 3, Vladimir Wrangel/AdobeStock; Page 5, Vladimir Wrangel/AdobeStock; Page 7, hradient/Pixabay; Page 9, the_lightwriter/Adobestock; Pages 10-11, NJ/AdobeStock; Page 13, cdownie/Pixabay; Page 15, WilliamCho/Pixabay; Page 17, Vladimir Wrangel/AdobeStock; Page 19, Hagit Berkovich/AdobeStock; Page 21, nataporn L/Shutterstock; Page 23; lonewolf6738/Pixabay; Page 25, nicoxuuhh/Pixabay; Page 27, YK/AdobeStock; Page 29, kamui29/AdobeStock; Page 31, alpe/AdobeStock; Page 33, nattanan726/Shutterstock

Table of Contents

What Are Fennec Foxes?

Fennec foxes are small mammals. They are the smallest kind of fox and smallest member of the **Canidae** family.

Fennec foxes are very **unique** in the **Canidae** family. They have many special **adaptations** that help them to survive in the desert.

2

Fennec foxes are usually a mix of cream, tan, black, white, and sandy brown in color.

Size

Fennec foxes are very small. They usually grow to be between nine and sixteen inches long. Their tail can add another twelve inches to their length.

When fully grown, fennec foxes usually weigh less than three pounds.

Male fennec foxes are usually
slightly larger than females.

Physical Characteristics

Fennec foxes use the color of their fur as **camouflage**. It helps them to blend in with the rocks and sand of their habitat.

Fennec foxes have very large ears. They can be between four and six inches long.

They help fennec foxes to hear

prey and predators from far

away.

Habitat

Fennec foxes are found in deserts. It is very hot where fennec foxes live. There is very little rainfall. It is too hot and dry for most animals to live there.

Fennec foxes are often seen around sand dunes, where they dig their burrows.

Range

Fennec foxes are found on the continents of Africa and Asia.

They are often seen in countries
like Egypt, Morocco, Niger,
Sudan, and Kuwait.

Diet

Fennec foxes are **omnivores**.

They eat both meat and

plants.

Their diet is made up of insects,

rodents, snails, plants, roots,

eggs, and lizards. Food can be

hard to find in the desert.

Fennec foxes are not **picky**

about what they eat.

Like other desert animals, fennec foxes drink very little water. They get most of their water from the food they eat.

Staying Cool

Fennec foxes pant when they get hot. This helps to release heat. Their fur is thick, which keeps them warm at night. The color **reflects** heat during the day, keeping them cool.

Their ears help fennec foxes to **regulate** their temperature. They do this by releasing heat.

Fennec foxes usually rest during

the day when it is the hottest.

They come out at night when it

is cooler.

Communication

Fennec foxes use mainly sound and scent to communicate with each other. They also play fight with members of their family group.

They have a special scent that they use to mark their **territory**. It tells other fennec foxes to stay away.

Fennec foxes use sounds such as barks, whimpers, and whines to communicate.

Movement

Fennec foxes have short legs, but they are able to move very fast. They have been known to run up to twenty miles per hour.

They are good at climbing, which helps them to look for and catch prey. They have been known to climb trees to find fruit to eat.

Fennec foxes are very good at digging. Their strong paws allow them to dig burrows quickly.

Fennec Fox Kits

Fennec foxes usually have a **litter** of between two and five babies. Their babies are called kits.

Mother fennec foxes stay with their kits while the fathers hunt for food. Kits are able to feed themselves by the time they are about five months old.

Kits are fully grown by the time they are about ten months old.

Fennec Fox Life

Fennec foxes use their strong paws to dig large burrows under the dirt. Their burrows are made up of many tunnels and **chambers** that are connected.

Fennec foxes are **nocturnal**. They are most active at night. They spend most of the day inside their burrow.

Fennec foxes come out of their burrows at night to hunt for food.

Social Life

Fennec foxes are very social animals. They spend a lot of time in groups of up to ten foxes.

A group of foxes is called a skulk or a leash. Fennec fox skulks are made up of families. They share a burrow and spend time together.

Fennec foxes play with their families. They also curl up together and rest.

Population

Fennec foxes are currently listed as **least concern**. They are not likely to become **endangered** in the near future.

It is not known how many fennec foxes live in the wild. They can be very hard for researchers to find and count.

In the wild, fennec foxes can

live up to about ten years. They

often live longer in zoos.

Fennec Foxes in Danger

Fennec foxes are facing several threats. The main threat is habitat destruction. Their habitats are being destroyed for roads, buildings, and farmland.

They are also hunted by people. Some are hunted for their fur. Others are caught to be sold and traded.

Wild fennec foxes are often caught and sold as pets.

Helping Fennec Foxes

Although fennec foxes are not **endangered**, people want to help them. They hope to keep fennec foxes from becoming **endangered** in the future.

In some places, special protected areas provide animals like fennec foxes with safe habitats.

In some countries, fennec foxes are protected animals. It is **illegal** to hunt or capture them.

Some groups focus on research and education. They want to learn about fennec foxes and teach others about them. They hope that people will want to help fennec foxes if they know more about them.

Glossary

Adaptation: a feature of an animal or plant helps it to survive

Camouflage: using color to blend in to the surroundings

Canidae: a family of animals that includes wolves, coyotes, dogs, and foxes

Chamber: room

Endangered: at risk of becoming extinct

Illegal: against the law

Least concern: when an animal is not likely to become endangered

Litter: a group of animals born at the same time

Nocturnal: animals that are active at night

Omnivore: an animal that eats meat and plants

Picky: fussy, hard to please

Reflect: to throw back from a surface

Regulate: to control

Territory: an area of land that an animal claims as its own

Unique: different, special

About the Author

Victoria Blakemore is a first grade

teacher in Southwest Florida with a

passion for reading.

You can visit her at

www.elementaryexplorers.com

Also in This Series

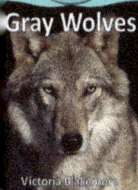

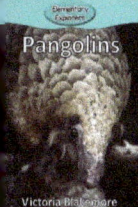

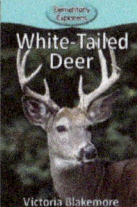

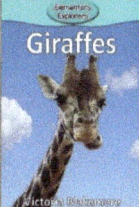

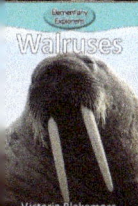

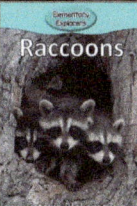

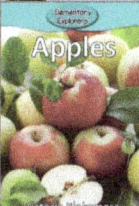

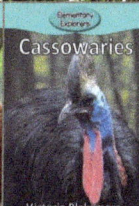

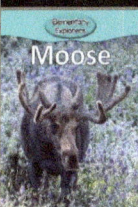

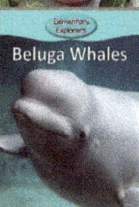

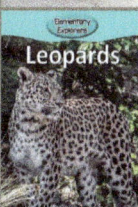

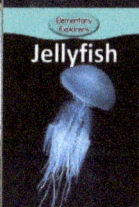

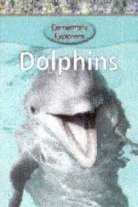

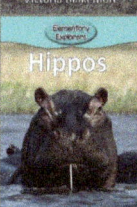

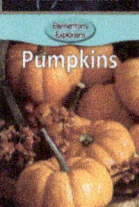

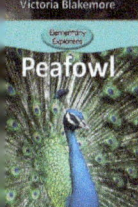

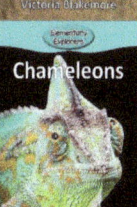

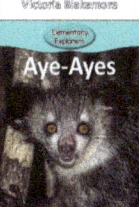

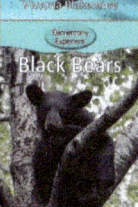

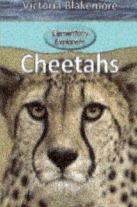

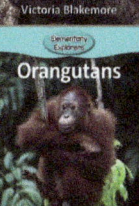

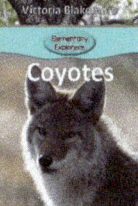

Gray Wolves	Sloths	Flamingos	Camels	Koalas	Honey Bees	Pandas
Pangolins	White-Tailed Deer	Orcas	Giraffes	Corn	Meerkats	Echidnas
Walruses	Raccoons	Bald Eagles	Apples	Arctic Foxes	Red Pandas	Cassowaries
Tigers	Ladybugs	Moose	Beluga Whales	Leopards	Elephants	Jellyfish
Binturongs	Lions	Dolphins	Reindeer	Hammerhead Sharks	Hippos	Pumpkins
Peafowl	Chameleons	Florida Panthers	Aye-Ayes	Black Bears	Cheetahs	Manatees
Gingerbread	Polar Bears	Hot Chocolate	Orangutans	Coyotes	Marshmallows	Strawberries

Elementary Explorers

Victoria Blakemore

Also in This Series

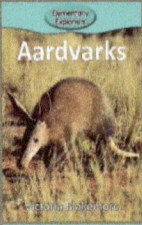

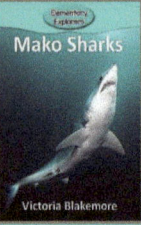

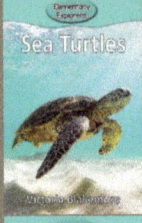

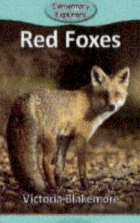

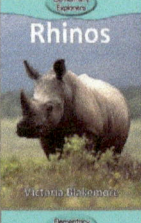

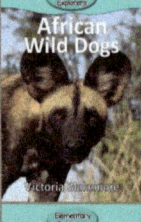

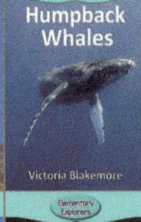

Elementary Explorers

Aardvarks	Mako Sharks	Alligators	Frogs	Hedgehogs	Brown Bears	Bongos
Sea Turtles	Quokkas	Muskrats	Zebras	Red Foxes	Ring-Tailed Lemurs	Platypuses
Anteaters	Kangaroos	Rhinos	Jaguars	Wombats	Capybaras	Gorillas
Cats	Skunks	Butterflies	Dingoes	Snow Leopards	African Wild Dogs	Penguins
Whale Sharks	Wolverines	Warthogs	Caracals	Badgers	Seals	Hummingbirds
Pikas	Humpback Whales	Pumas	Lemonade	Llamas	Tulips	Ostriches
Sunflowers	Fennec Foxes	Sea Lions	Squirrels	Roses	Porcupines	Ice Cream

Victoria Blakemore

www.ingramcontent.com/pod-product-compliance
Lightning Source LLC
Chambersburg PA
CBHW051251020426
42333CB00025B/3159